Kitty n Rover
A moral in every story

Sunita Mathew

BLUEROSE PUBLISHERS
India | U.K.

Copyright © Sunita Mathew 2023

All rights reserved by author. No part of this publication may be reproduced, stored in a retrieval system or transmitted in any form or by any means, electronic, mechanical, photocopying, recording or otherwise, without the prior permission of the author. Although every precaution has been taken to verify the accuracy of the information contained herein, the publisher assumes no responsibility for any errors or omissions. No liability is assumed for damages that may result from the use of information contained within.

BlueRose Publishers takes no responsibility for any damages, losses, or liabilities that may arise from the use or misuse of the information, products, or services provided in this publication.

For permissions requests or inquiries regarding this publication, please contact:

BLUEROSE PUBLISHERS
www.BlueRoseONE.com
info@bluerosepublishers.com
+91 8882 898 898
+4407342408967

ISBN: 978-93-5989-976-3

Cover design: Sunita Mathew
Typesetting: Rohit

First Edition: December 2023

Preface

These are the stories I made up for my daughter when she was 3 to 4 yrs ,There was a book on animals that I was showing her that would amaze her a lot , In the evening we would go to the park which had a lot of trees and a lot of greenery every time she would imagine an animal there ,we would pretend and discuss about the animal ,it would make her feel like we are in an adventure in the jungle,, that night I would make up a story about that animal which made her happy and, she always loved the stories , 10 yrs later she remembers them all now ,so when I am writing she reminds me which story should I write and corrects me, after writing every story I make her read to check if I have made some mistakes that is the power of our children's memory, they remember everything we have told them good and bad

When I told her these stories, she knew animals don't talk but communicate with actions to humans but it was so much fun to see her smile and hug and kiss me before sleeping

She always asked me what was the moral of this story and I had to make up something or the other

The moral of my stories are to let them know that there should be no fear in us if we are doing the right thing but only fear God as he is watching us all the time because he loves us.

And children enjoy these stories its not real but a lot of fun .

These stories are about animals who been taken out of zoos and circuses when they become old or sick as nobody wants to look after them ,there are animals who have got lost as their homes have been destroyed due to deforestation for humans needs.Each one has a different story and there are a few other stories which I have enjoyed writing I hope you'll love reading it too.

Characters - Simona , Aviah
Babu watchman
Robby-Blind boy
Animals names
Jumbo- Elephant
Bella- Hippo
Sonu and Monu - monkeys
Gaffu - Giraffe
Stripy - Zebra
Simba -Lion
Kitty-Cat
Rover-Dog
Eagu-Eagle

Contents

Animals in the park 1

Diamond necklace 4

Bella's hiphop 9

King of the jungle 13

Circle of life 17

The eagles and the squirells 20

The blind boy 24

Saving the mouse 29

You are special 31

Kindness Pays 36

Mothers Love 40

Animal Facts 45

Animals in the park

Simona and her friends were all excited they were going to the park because they had got the news that animals were going to be introduced into the park, somebody had just read a notice but they wanted to make sure the news was true .They knew Kitty the cat and Roger the dog in the park and they loved them very much.

When they reached they tried reading the notice board put on the gate but it was too high so they went to the watch man Bablu and asked him," Is it true , Bablu just nodded with a big smile on his face and told them today an elephant is going to be becoming from the zoo,,all the children just jumped with joy,just then Kitty and Roger came ,all the children jumped and went running to them,they looked very worried.

"What's the matter are you'll not happy " Simona asked them they replied today an elephant and tomorrow a giraffe and a hippo are coming , should we not be worried , the children started laughing no you'll should not be worried ,they would be more worried and you'll two could welcome them make them welcome here as you'll two are the hosts of this park,

They still looked worried ,just then the gate was being opened and Bablu was calling them close ,the children pushed Kitty and Roger in front to welcome the elephant ,just then the trailer was opened and the elephant came out he was lead into the park and released , he looked huge but he came close to Kitty and Rover and just patted them both on their heads and came close to the children and just sat down in front of them and said hello. The children all came close and started touching and hugging him.

Everybody was happy he told them they called him Jumbo in the zoo so that they could call him Jumbo then the children told him tomorrow a giraffe and Hippo was coming to the park ,he saw they looked worried so he told them they eat leaves and fruits not little children so no worries, everybody started laughing,Kitty took Jumbo around the park and told him all about the park timings of when the humans were around and where his food would be served and asked him to choose where he wanted to rest and sleep.Jumbo was very happy because this was so much better then the Zoo.Now all of them were excited to meet the giraffe and he Hippo , Next day very early in the morning they were released into the park,Jumbo. Kitty welcomed them and made them comfortable the giraffe was shy but the hippo was very friendly,she asked question and spoke nonstop but Kitty fell in love with her and later became her best friend.

They had no names as they had come from a forest which was no more one because of deforestation, so Kitty named the Hippo " "Bella" and the others decided to call the giraffe " Gaffu ". Like this more animals joined the group like "Strippy"the Zebra , Sonu and Monu the monkeys , Eagu the eagle and more and more and they all lived harmoniously.

M/S-

Diamond necklace

It was celebration time at the park as it was Bella's birthday ,all the animals had asked their friends (Simona and Aviah) to get her a cake as Bella loved chocolate cake.Every body was busy at getting her a gift as she took a lot of trouble to give every body gifts, and each one had to get a different gift

not one common gift,so the stress level was too much and all wanted to go for her party because there were games ,snacks and lots of fun at her parties.

Everybody met in the afternoon to show each other their gifts Jumbo had got her a bag made out

Of leaves, somebody had definitely helped him,Gaffu the giraffe had got her a bunch of flowers,

Sonu,Monu the monkeys had got her a bunch of balloons,Kitty the cat got her a bowl which she had got from somebody and like this every body had got her something,all wanted to see what the

Others had got her.

In the evening Simona had asked the watchman Babu to play some music,By six everybody had gathered,Simona and her friends got her the cake, every body gave Bella their gifts she was so

Happy but when they asked her to cut the cake she refused because her friend Eagu the eagle was not there yet,just then he flew in and he had something shiny in his beak ,it was shining a lot,when he came closer they all saw it was a beautiful necklace for Bella she loved it as soon as she saw it and wore it immediately ,it was shinning and looked good on her ,she loved jewellery, the party was a hit and everybody enjoyed as soon as the

Sun set all wished her again and said goodbye .

The next day as people started walking in the park,the animals were still resting but Bella came out of her little home and was walking proudly with her necklace on, the old people were admiring it and giving her a lot of compliments ,even all the ladies were noticing it , all the animals were laughing saying it is too early in the day to wear something so shiny but Bella could not be bothered

But one lady kept staring at Bella's necklace suddenly she started making a call and asked somebody to come to the park ,

The animals had started playing and suddenly Babu the watch man called out to Bella ,after sometime there was a commotion and Jumbo and Gaffu saw the police and a lady screaming they were quite shocked at the crowd that had gathered so they went to check with Bella what was the chaos about ,they noticed Bella was crying and ,when they checked with Bella she said "This necklace belonged to this lady apparently it was stolen from her" ,she was trying to explain to the police I have not robbed it ,it was gift to me by my friend ,

That's when Jumbo told the police that Eagu the eagle had given the necklace to Bella for her birthday ,the police was finding everything so strange they did not know whether to laugh or get angry, they told Jumbo and all the animals that necklace was a diamond necklace worth 20 lakhs and

whoever has robbed this would go to jail.all the animals got scared that Bella would go to jail but Jumbo told them to stop worrying ,he whistled loudly looking up at the sky every body was shocked to hear the loud whistle but suddenly the eagle came flying down and sat on Jumbo ,he noticed his friend Bella was crying bitterly,Jumbo asked him where did you get the necklace from , he looked surprised and just pointed to the skyscraper which was two buildings away ,and he told every body he found It lying on the window sill on the top floor it was so shiny and beautifull, I thought,Bella would love it ,it was lying there for a whole day and there was a lot of shiny things so nobody would miss one going away everybody started laughing ,the Police understood that these animals and birds had no idea about the value to them they were not diamonds just shiny stones ,

Jumbo realised how the mistake could have happened and made all the animals understand how we

Can't take anything that belongs to others ,they all looked very surprised a they shared everything

Nothing in the park belonged to one of them but to all ,he then came and returned the necklace and told the ladies that we are ignorant animals so please forgive us .The lady who the necklace belonged to was so surprised but she first turned around and told the police to go away saying it was all a misunderstanding then she turned around and told the animals you'll are not ignorant we are ignorant,

giving so much importance to material things that we forget other people or animals emotions ,so I am sorry for getting the police and creating such a commotion . she said sorry to Bella and said something in Eagus ears and walked away.

All the animals felt sorry for Bella but did not say anything, she just walked away with tears in her eyes to her house ,Eagu said something in Jumbos ears and flew away ,Jumbo called all the animals and informed them to meet outside Bella's house in the evening saying let's do something to make her feel good ,they were clueless but they knew Jumbo had a plan.

In the evening it was beautiful the sun was setting and there was a cool breeze swaying the leaves on the trees, all met outside her home , Bella was the only one who had a cute little home where all the animals who felt sick would go to her and she would make medicine from leaves and roots and give them they always got better.,they all loved her a lot.

Jumbo knocked on her door ,when she opened her door she came out and smiled at them saying she was perfectly alright, she had forgotten about the necklace so stop feeling bad and let's play ,they all knew she was lying just then Jumbo whistled and then Eagu came soaring down and he had something shinny in his beak not 1 but 2 necklaces he gave them to Bella and said the lady who the necklace belonged had called him and given these to give it to you , she was quite shocked she slowly took them and asked "hope the police will not come again, she wore them, it was more colourful and shiny she looked and said I love them and now I have 2 ,all were so happy for her and thanked God for the generosity of that lady and blessed her .

MOS-Never take anything that belongs to others because it will never give you happiness or peace of mind.

Bella's hiphop

Bella the hippo had just returned after a walk in the park with Kitty the cat. She loved spending time with Kitty, who knew a lot about things that happened outside the park.

Her house in the corner of the park was a cosy little place. Bella was the only animal with a home in the park; everybody came there if they were sad, hungry, or hurt. She was the best; she took care of every animal in the park.

Bella was just getting ready to leave for dinner with the others when she heard moaning and crying. She looked up as she had no roof, just a tree covering her tiny home. She heard the sound again and called out, "Who is there? Please come out. Everything will be alright."

That's when she saw the monkey. She knew it was a very young one. She called out again, "Please, come down."

He climbed down slowly and landed in Bella's arms. She set him down and then saw he was hurt on the head and in many places on his body. Before checking on his wounds, she asked him, "Are you hungry?"

He vigorously nodded, so she gave him a banana and some other fruits. While he was eating, she cleaned his wounds, put some medicine, and bandaged him up.

There was a knock on her door, and she saw Jumbo outside. She went out with the now-cheerful monkey, looking like a wounded soldier. He was holding on to Bella. Jumbo looked confused, so Bella explained.

When they were seated with all the animals, the monkey saw how loving and kind everybody was and started crying. That's when Sonu and Monu, the monkeys from the park, recognised and said, "This is the monkey the man has been asking the watchman about. His monkey has been missing."

When the young monkey heard this, he started crying and hid behind Bella. She picked him up and asked, "Did this man hurt you? The monkey told them about how he had been treated. He took him to the beach every evening to dance in front of people so he could collect money. But he would beat him and keep him hungry if the money were not enough.

The animals knew they had to do something. After they discussed the plan, it was immediately put into action, and the watchman was informed.

The following day when the park opened, the watchman saw that the man had returned, saying he was sure his monkey was in the park. He was asked to come in, but all the animals were standing there, so he panicked. Then he saw three monkeys. He came closer and shouted, pointing out to the bandaged monkey and saying it was his. That's when Bella asked him how he was hurt so much.

The man laughed, saying, "He is very naughty and falls a lot."

As he went closer, the monkey started crying and hid behind Bella. The man went to snatch him, but all the animals stood in front of Bella. Simba roared, so the man got scared and stopped immediately.

That's when Simona, their friend, walked into the park with the police and informed them about the torture this little monkey had gone through because of this man. The police took him away and warned him never to return to the park.

Everybody was so happy, and all hugged Simona and thanked her for helping them as she was always there for the animals with the help of other adults. The monkey was named Hiphop by Bella and was loved by all the others, but Bella was his Mamma.

Moral of the story: Humans need to learn how to love unconditionally from animals.

King of the jungle

The animals were always very excited whenever a new animal was introduced in the park, but the news of a lion coming was not very happy news. Jumbo remembered the lions in the circus, who were not friendly, but he did not want to tell the other animals because most were already scared. Kitty said, "There has never been a lion in this park. Even the humans would get scared, but the humans are bringing him here, so maybe he would not be so bad." They could only wait and pray he was a friendly lion.

They were ready to welcome him the following day as that was the only choice. A huge vehicle came near the gate, and three people got down. They opened the door of the truck and carefully brought the lion out. They slowly directed him towards the gate and let him go. Everybody watched him; he ambled in and stretched a little as he was stuck in the big vehicle for a long time. He looked around and suddenly saw all the animals and was shocked. All of them slowly came towards him.

Jumbo went ahead and said, "Hello! How was the journey, and are you happy getting out of your cage?"

The lion came forward and rubbed himself against Jumbo's legs and said, "Are you saying I won't be in a cage anymore?"

Jumbo said, "No, we all are never in cages. We walk freely here."

He was happy, but he had a lot of questions. Everyone was so friendly. Kitty the cat and Bella the hippo had answers for everything.

He told them he was too old and could no longer stay at the zoo. He thought they would put him to sleep, but he was happy to be at the park. He wanted to live and go back to his home in the jungle. Nobody wanted to tell him there was no more jungle to return to, so it was better he remained ignorant.

They named him SIMBA; he liked it very much. He got used to the park life and was very happy. Nobody stared at him when he went for a walk with other animals.

One evening, he had just woken up and wanted water, which was outside the bushy area. While he was drinking water, he heard a child crying. He knew he was not ready for the humans at the park, but he loved children. Simba looked around and approached the little girl, asking her, "What's wrong, my dear?"

The girl stopped crying, looked at him with awe, and said, "Wow, lion!"

"Yes, I am Simba, the new lion here. But why were you crying?"

She hesitantly told him, "My mother works in that building, pointing out to the building in front of the park. She can't take me there and drops me off in the park for one hour. But there is a boy who comes exactly then, and he troubles me. He is not a good boy. He frightens me by saying if I tell anybody, he will hurt my mom."

Simba was shocked; no animal would hurt a child. Then what kind of monster was this? He asked her where the boy was. She said he would arrive anytime. Simba told her, "You sit here, and I will hide behind you in the bushes. When he comes, I will frighten him, so don't worry."

After some time, the boy came with another boy and started pulling her hair. They pushed her around, making her sit on the ground and pinching her cheeks. She started crying. They laughed at her, and then one made her sit on his lap. She was crying bitterly, but they kept laughing.

Simba could not wait any longer. He came out from behind the bushes and roared so loudly that the whole park heard it. Everyone ran toward the sound as they had never heard Simba roar so loudly , but the boys jumped up panicked and ran away.

The girl was so happy she hugged Simba tightly, not letting go. When the animals and the people came close, they saw a little girl hugging Simba. All of them stopped and stared at them in wonder.

She stopped hugging and kissing Simba, climbed on his back, and hugged him again.

Simba said, "Nobody will ever hurt you in this park again."

He walked towards all the animals and introduced his new friend, Maya, to them. The humans there looked at the lion and little girl and started clapping. They had never seen anything so beautiful.

Moral of the story: Tell somebody your problems , there is always a Simba in your life too , be brave.

Circle of life

One evening, Jumbo the elephant and Gaffu the giraffe were sitting away from the central area of the park, which was crowded with many people. They were just watching everyone pass by.

Suddenly Gaffu said, "Some look happy, some look sad, some look worried, and some look stressed. And, like us, some are just sitting and looking at others passing by. So many emotions, but I wonder what's happening in their lives."

Jumbo started laughing and said, "You are from the jungle. I was in a circus. Humans are strange creatures. What you see is not what you get. The ones you think are happy might not be, the ones you think are listening to their friends might be thinking about their problems, and those who laugh you should worry about as you don't know whether they are laughing at the joke or laughing at you. They are very complex."

Gaffu looked confused. "What do you mean by that? Don't they have emotions like us?"

Jumbo answered, "We are animals that show emotions when hurt, hungry, scared, or want to show love. We don't hide anything—it is what it is. We don't pretend. We don't show false emotions. We are not cruel or unkind unless threatened, but it's different here, as humans can be cruel sometimes. I was mistreated in the circus. The sad part was I did not know for what."

Gaffu looked sad, so Jumbo immediately said, "All is not bad; look at those children playing there. They are pure. You will know what they are going through just by glancing at their faces."

Gaffu did not look relieved, so Jumbo knew he had to say something more, or Gaffu would be upset for a long time.

So, he started, "You know this park belongs to the humans, right, and they are sharing it with us. It's good of them. I was brought to this park by a kind man who saw me in a bad state in the zoo. So there are a lot of kind people in this world. Also, they bring food for us, so it's not that bad; there are good people too."

That's when Kitty the cat and Rover the dog rushed over looking very disturbed ,they looked a little scared too, so Jumbo immediately got up to see what the problem was, but Kitty said, "No, there is no problem here. We were walking outside when we saw a big van taking all the dogs they could catch. It was frightening, so we ran into the park."

Gaffu looked at Jumbo because he was confused by this act of human cruelty. After all, according to him, this world belonged to all humans and animals.

Jumbo thought for some time and then said, "There are at least twenty dogs on every street, and they are a menace in the city, don't you agree, Rover?"

Rover sadly nodded his head. Jumbo continued, "We have some lovely people who feed dogs on the streets, and some help those who are hurt. But most dogs are just growing lazy and sometimes violent. If you were in the jungle, you'd have been eaten or attacked by now. Hence, it is the circle of life; People are very friendly to us. They bring food for us in the park, so we can't complain if some of us disturb their daily lives. It's our fault, as the city belongs to them."

By this time, all the animals were surrounding Jumbo and Gaffu, and they all looked like they understood. But Jumbo knew this topic was complex, so he told them, "Stop worrying and be happy." He looked into the skies and said, "Remember this always—God loves all his creations, and we all are important to him."

All the animals seemed very relieved, and all felt a little better.

Moral of the story: There is good and evil in the world but its what we choose that matters.

The eagles and the squirells

One afternoon, Jumbo was relaxing and chatting with Gaffu the giraffe. They were at the back of the park because they needed a lot of space to sit. It was afternoon, and the park was empty and silent. So, all the animals took a nap. Suddenly, the monkeys Sonu and Monu jumped down from the trees. Jumbo glared at them.

They immediately said, "Sorry, we just had to tell you that Toni, the squirrel living on the tree next to Simona's building, was talking to us. He has a big problem and wants you to help them, Jumbo."

Jumbo immediately awoke from his slumber and said, "Please call him. We will help, but tell him to come before people enter the park."

Sonu and Monu immediately bounded off to call Toni. Jumbo thought it would take them some time, so he shut his eyes, wondering what problem a squirrel could have. Suddenly, he heard some noise. He opened his eyes and was shocked because there was not one squirrel but hundreds of them. It was like a carpet on the floor of the park. Gaffu and Jumbo started laughing.

Toni came forward and said, "We are having a problem. We are having a shortage of food because some birds are attacking us. They don't even eat the fruits from that tree. They just attack us, grab the fruit, fly away, and drop it somewhere far. We tried talking to them, but they come in groups, so we can't fight back."

Jumbo was surprised because he knew birds were not the kind to do this unless they had a reason. He had to find out more about this. Hence, he enquired, "Why are they doing this knowing you are in such significant numbers? I can't believe some birds are frightening you."

Toni explained, "We gather at the top of these high trees early in the morning to eat and drink water from the dew on the leaves. It is right on top, so we don't disturb anyone. But these birds come in great numbers, and their beaks are very sharp."

Jumbo knew that no animal attacked another unless he was hungry. He knew that he had to do something to help the squirrels. He called out to Eagu the eagle, who appeared momentarily. Eagu said he would do something tomorrow morning.

The next day at six in the morning, all the squirrels gathered on top of the tree. They were busy eating and drinking when a swarm of birds suddenly descended and started bothering them. Suddenly, they saw an eagle sitting nearby who asked them, "Why are you doing this to these poor squirrels?"

The birds turned around and laughed, "We are just playing with them."

There was a loud sound from above, and the birds turned to see a flock of eagles flying straight to the tops of all the trees. The birds got scared, knowing that eagles rarely flew so low. The eagles landed on the trees and started pecking the smaller birds, who then started flying away.

Eagu flew towards them, saying, "They are just playing with you. Do you like it? If we see you attacking the squirrels again, we will attack you."

The birds immediately flew away, knowing they could not return to this park.

The animals watched the show from the ground and laughed when the smaller birds flew away. Eagu and the other eagles saw all the animals looking happy and clapping for them. They were glad they could help the animals and flew away.

The squirrels came down to thank Jumbo and the others. They were delighted.

Jumbo said, "You can come here any time." Then he turned to the rest of the animals.

"In the jungle, we hunt and eat. Not in the city where there is food for all. But we must learn to share, as God worries about each of us. I would understand if the birds were fighting to get food for themselves. But I could not allow them to trouble others. Live and let live."

Moral of the story: If your actions make somebody unhappy, stop.

The blind boy

One beautiful evening, the park was noisy and full of children playing as it was a weekend. All the animals were relaxing in their corners as some children, especially the boys, were quite naughty and rough while handling the animals. So, the animals tried not to interact with them.

Kitty the cat and Rover the dog were quite brave and would sometimes linger around the children. That evening, Kitty was sleeping on the bench, and Rover was sleeping under it. Suddenly, Kitty heard somebody talking, so she opened her eyes. A lady was guiding a little boy to sit on the bench. He was wearing dark glasses. He must have been around ten years old. Kitty found it strange as the boy was old enough that he did not need to be looked after and also noticed the boy looked so sad.

Just then, Rover got up and came out, stretching. When he noticed the boy, he said, "Hi, Robby, how are you?"

The boy knew Rover and started patting his head, and suddenly he had a big smile. He introduced Robby to Kitty, who sat beside him on the bench. Kitty came close to him and rubbed herself against his hand. He said, "Hello," and rubbed her head, too. Kitty loved it.

After some time, the lady told Robby, "It's getting late. Let's go." He stood up quietly, held her hand, and said goodbye to Kitty and Rover.

Kitty was so surprised to see him go walking sadly with the lady. Rover turned around and told Kitty that Robby was blind.

"He lives in the next building. When his parents go to work, he has a nurse that looks after him. Don't worry. His parents love him a lot. When he hears other children play, he misses playing with them, and that's why he looks sad. Otherwise, his parents do many things with him."

Kitty thought for some time and then went straight to Jumbo and Bella, who were good at finding solutions to problems. When they heard the problem, Bella immediately knew what to do.

As it was Sunday the next day, Rover went to Robby's building as his mother always fed the dogs in their building. He went up to her and told her the plan. She was very excited and agreed to bring Robby to the park in the evening.

Everything was planned. All the animals knew what to do, so Rover was not worried about anything, as everybody was doing it out of love for the little boy. Bella told everybody what they had to do and explained his lack of vision, so they had to take care of the little boy.

When Robby and his mother entered the park in the evening, Kitty and Rover went over. Then all the other animals came out. The mother was so shocked, but Robby noticed there was no sound of children screaming and playing.

He asked his mother, "Have you brought me to a different park?"

She said, "No, it's the same park, but today it is closed to others. It is only open for you as all the animals wanted to meet you as they know you love animals."

Robby was so excited. He heard an elephant trumpet, and then Jumbo touched his hands with his trunk. Kitty told Robby, "Do not worry. Jumbo is going to lift you and put you on his back. We will walk around and describe the park to you."

Robby was so excited. After that, the monkeys Sonu and Monu lifted him into the trees and explained what could be seen in the distance.

Then Gaffu told him, "I am a young giraffe, so I can't take you very high, but I am the fastest. Do you want to sit on my back? You just hold me tight as I have a long neck."

Everybody looked at Robby's mother, who smiled and said, "Go for it."

Robby was so excited as all the animals followed them. He laughed so much, and his mother had tears in her eyes. Afterwards, they went to Bella's house, where she gave him something sweet to eat, telling his mother it was natural from the flowers and plants.

The mother laughed, saying, "I have never seen my son so happy. I am not worried."

All the animals came to play with Robby. At the end of the beautiful day, Robby's mother said, "He is going for an operation tomorrow. Please pray for him. If the procedure is successful, he will at least have seventy-five percent vision."

All the animals promised to pray that Robby had a successful surgery.

One week passed, but nobody had heard about Robby. He had to come back from Hyderabad, where the hospital was. They kept asking Rover to check again, but there was no news.

Then, one evening when the animals were in their corners waiting for everyone to leave, they heard somebody screaming. Everyone turned to look. It was

Robby screaming and running towards them. They were all so happy to see him and rushed towards him.

However, they got worried when they saw he was still wearing dark glasses. His mother explained that he had to wear them for another week, but the operation was successful. They stopped and stared at him. He first hugged Kitty and Rover before hugging and naming them all as he remembered all their names.

Robby said, "I was waiting to thank you all for the lovely time. That memory will never leave me." The mother had gotten all the animals some food and said, "If you need anything, just ask Robby. We will try to help."

All the animals were so happy and could not wait for Robby to return to the park and play with the other children.

Moral of the story: You can be blind by lacking sight or be blind by lacking a heart. To have a friend be a friend.

Saving the mouse

It was a rainy day, and a mouse was having difficulty looking for food for her little ones. But she could not stop as they were starving, so she kept wandering in search of something to eat.

Suddenly, she saw a massive gate, so she entered and realised it was a park. As she walked through the park, she saw a pond and carefully moved towards it. She saw a dog sitting under a tree and approached him.

"Hello, can you help me to find some food for my children as I can't see much in this rain?" The dog looked up and saw a very wet mouse and started laughing. "I don't have food for myself, so where do I get food for you?"

But he felt bad for the mouse and knew he had to help, so he started thinking about a plan. He told her to wait under the tree and went looking for food for the mouse. On his way, he met Jumbo and told him he was looking for food for a mouse and her children. Jumbo laughed too, but he knew he had to help the mouse and her children. Rover and Jumbo began thinking about a plan.

After some time, Bella the hippo joined them in discussing the problem. She suggested she would take them home, but they had no idea where the mouse lived and how to get all her children to the park. Suddenly, Jumbo whistled, and Eagu the eagle swooped down. Jumbo requested him to take the mouse and bring her family back to the park, but Bella had a better idea. She went and got a basket and tied it around Eagu. While this was happening, Rover went to fetch the mouse.

When the mouse arrived, she was scared of seeing so many animals, but Rover made her feel comfortable and told her they were solving her problems. She panicked more at getting into the basket but thought about her hungry children in the rain. She immediately got in and gave directions to where her children were. Because it was not too far, she could get all her five children to the park.

Bella had a cosy place where there was no rain. She had made it nice and warm. She gave them food, especially the mother, who needed it the most.

And as she was now going to live in the park, they named her Molly because she was part of the family.

Molly was so happy that her children were dry, fed, and warm. She realised helping one another was so important, and she promised always to be helpful to others.

Moral of the story: Help one another always.

You are special

One evening, all the animals gathered to have dinner. Bella shared what she had cooked; the rest came with goodies too. Kitty always got some food from outside the park. Gaffu the giraffe had some leaves to share with Stripey the zebra. But Stripey was missing, and Gaffu had not seen him all day.

Gaffu asked, "Have you seen Stripey anywhere?" Everybody shook their heads negatively—even Kitty, who always knew where everyone was.

Jumbo, the eldest of the group, started thinking and said, "Yesterday, when there were many children around, the boys were chasing Stripey. But he is a fast runner, so I did not think it was a problem."

Jumbo ordered the rest of the animals to search the park. As it was huge, he made them go in all directions. He even trumpeted and called Eagu the eagle. As soon as Eagu soared down from the sky, Jumbo told him to keep an eye out for Stripey as he would get an aerial view. After a good hour, Eagu returned and told Jumbo, "He is hiding behind the bushes in the centre of the park. He is just lying down there."

Jumbo immediately sent Sonu and Monu the monkeys to look for Stripey. They went into the bushes and shook the zebra. "Are you okay? What's wrong? Everybody is worried."

Stipey shook his head and said, "I am okay, so leave me alone."

They did not leave, telling him to come and tell Jumbo, who was very angry. Stripey was scared of Jumbo, so he got up and came out of the bushes.

Everybody was relieved to see him, but Jumbo looked angry and asked, "What's wrong? Why are you hiding in the bushes?"

That's when Stripey started crying and said, "Everybody makes fun of my stripes. They throw stones at me too. It's embarrassing when they do it in front of everyone. They make fun of my stripes, so I want to eliminate them."

The other animals looked shocked. Bella said, "You are beautiful and different. Why would you want to have our dull colours?"

But Stripey would not listen. After thinking for some time, Jumbo said he would sort it out. Everybody wondered what he was planning to do. When Simona and her friends came to play in the morning, Jumbo asked her to buy some dark brown colour with a big brush and even told her what it was for.

They got two boxes of colour and asked Stripey to come to Bella's house the next day. Everybody was curious, but Jumbo took him to a corner with a bucket full of colour and started pouring it on him. Sonu and Monu took care that the colour didn't splash anywhere else. They took him out to dry when it was done and asked if he liked the colour.

He was so happy, but everyone else looked shocked. But Jumbo had told them not to say anything, so they kept silent. That evening when the park opened, people started coming. Stripey was sitting near Kitty.

Suddenly, a group of children approached Kitty and asked her, "Where is the zebra? And why are you sitting with this donkey?" Kitty remained quiet, so the boys went away.

When they met at night, the animals said, "Everybody was asking for you, Stripey. Some had come with cameras to take your photo, not ours."

Just then, Jumbo said, "We must give you a new name, as we can't call you Stripey. It does not suit you now, so choose a new name." The animals waited for Stripey to answer.

He looked sad and said, "Nobody looked at me at all today, and the children who saw me called me a donkey. I don't want to be a donkey but a zebra, so my dear friends, how do I get rid of this colour?"

Jumbo looked at him angrily and asked, "Should we all worry about how you look and feel all the time? I want to complain about my long trunk. Why do I need to breathe with this? Bella wants to be slimmer. Gaffu does not like his long neck. I could go on, but we all are grateful to the creator for how we look and our sizes, as he knows best." Saying that, Jumbo turned and walked away.

The others stayed with Stripey as he was crying, and he kept apologising to all of them.

He just sat there, but Bella told everyone to come out and wait until Jumbo returned. They were comforting Stripey when Bella suddenly screamed, "Get back."

Everyone was shocked because Jumbo had dragged out a hose with water gushing out. He aimed at Stripey, and everybody laughed as they saw the water was making his colour come out.

Kitty said, "It was water colour, so we knew it would come out with water. We also knew you would not be happy."

Stripey joined in the laughter, realising what Jumbo said was true; just be satisfied with how the creator has made you.

Moral of the story: Be happy and love yourself. You are special.

Kindness Pays

It was beautiful day ,the park was pretty silent as the people had finished their walks and their daily exercise and most of them had to go to work or had other things to do ,the only sound was the incessant sound of the traffic outside the park ,some of the animals woke up early but some waited for all the humans to leave , as the animals meal was served near the watchman's cabin they all came one by one to have their breakfast Jumbo, Bella were the earliest ,then slowly all of them, they started with thanking God and blessing everybody who were providing them with the food.

But they all ate slowly and waited for everybody so that they could have a chat , after sometime Kitty realized Sonu and Monu were not around, Gaffu had the longest neck so he went to check on him he returned back immediately with Monu , who looked worried and said 'Sonu has not been well all night and he looks very weak, Bella immediately took a banana and started going towards the tree everybody followed ,they realized he had to be brought down from the tree Monu went up woke him up and asked him to get on Jumbos back ,looking at him they realized they could not do anything about it ,they called the watchman and asked him to call their friend Simona ,but he turned and said there was no reply ,they got really worried but Bella kept feeding him the banana which she had mashed so that it was easy for him to eat .

Kitty looked around and saw an old man sitting on the bench looking pensive and in his own thoughts ,but Kitty bravely went up to him and told him the problem ,and how all the animals were worried did not know what to do he thought for a long time and looked at them pretty shocked But then his driver came to pick him up so he just got up and walked away, all the animals saw what happened and were sad he was probably a rich man and no time for such trivial matters ,,they all thought for some time and then Rover went and told Babu the watch man about it but he had nobody's number to call who were responsible nor the number of the Zoo ,they sat around Sonu and kept thinking who to go to, Bella checked his temperature so put some cold compression on him but knew she could not do anything else .they all sat sadly and worried but Kitty and Rover went outside the park to find help .

It was 11 in the morning by then and suddenly kitty came running back happily saying the ambulance is here and the Vets are come to take him ,everything was really swift ,they came checked him and told the animals we need to take him to the clinic he was lifted on a stretcher and was being carried out but Monu told them he needs to go with them , so both were taken away ,it happened so quick the animals all were shocked and was wondering how this happened but the mystery was solved because the old man's driver had come back to tell them it his boss who had arranged the ambulance and the vets to come , they were surprised because they thought he looked like he did not care but peoples kindness always surprised them .

They all were just waiting for some news but were happy that Sonu would be in good hands because they were aware if they were in the wild it would be different but they were domesticated so the food they ate and habits they had was different but it was only in the evening Sonu and Monu came back ,Sonu was much better ,it was some food poisoning so was very dehydrated but now he had to be careful and eat only fruits.

Everything was back to normal that evening they sat in Simba's area as nobody went in there so it was verry private but Kitty and Rover went to find the old man to thank him even Jumbo and Bella followed when they went up kitty went first and thanked him for his kindness and Kitty asked him if Jumbo and Bella could meet him when he agreed they came Jumbo bowed down and touched his feet but kitty stopped Bella from hugging him just in case he was fearful but they all thanked him ,they looked at him ,he had tears in his eyes and after some time he told them " I am very sick but I only have my driver and nurse who looks after me ,my children are all busy and have no time it was so heartwarming when I heard you'll were just worried about a monkey who was not related to you'll but was just your friend I was so touched ,I did it for selfish reasons as I want friends like you'll " suddenly Bella jumped and hugged hard ,the old man started laughing it was a heart touching moment he even told them the Vet would come every month to check them.

All the animals were glad to hear this ,soon Sonu started jumping from branch to branch of the trees and life went on happily.

MS – Be kind to everyone because it always comes back .

Mothers Love

It was a beautiful evening ,the sun had just started setting and the skies had a beautiful orange colour ,it was getting a little bit cooler too .The animals loved it because the sun was too hot for them ,all the animals were sitting together in the corner of the park waiting for all the people to leave ,only kitty was missing . they asked Rover If he had any idea where she was but he answered negatively .

They loved waiting for her to have dinner because she had all the news from outside ,some good some not so good some very bad but unless it affected them it was just news.

Suddenly they heard Babu calling out to them and Kitty was with him so they all gathered around them , Today the news was another elephant was coming to the park they all were shocked because 2 elephants in the park was too much but as they could not do anything about it but just wait and watch to see what was going to happen Jumbo knowing they were all worried just said

"Don't worry it can't be that bad ,maybe we will like him or her too "

Next day all the animals were eagerly waiting near the gate ,just then the gate opened and the vehicle entered ,when the door opened they were shocked to see a little elephant enter the park ,he looked confused and scared but he bravely walked towards them and said my name is Appu , I have come from the zoo which took me 3 hours and was very uncomfortable ride , Bella went and hugged him first and then everyone said hello " But he kept staring at Jumbo who slowly came towards him and tapped him on his head with his trunk suddenly he started crying ,all were very surprised and Jumbo asked him what was wrong.

He sniffling loudly said he was missing his mother , on questioning him ,they found out his mother was taken to a circus very far away and they had left him behind in the zoo , they all felt sad but could not do anything so just made him comfortable and gave him something to eat But Jumbo asked Kitty and Rover to find out what the real story was, After checking with Babu who knew everything about the animals who had no idea as well but he said he would check too.

The next day Appu was out and ready to play he just rolled on the grass and toppled all over ,Bella was enjoying it too she rolled with him while the other animals just watched them with a smile on their face , just then Rover joined them with Simona their friend who was so excited to meet Appu but he just ,rolled his trunk round her arm and tried to pull her to play she started laughing out loud but just unwound his trunk and went to speak to Jumbo ,she told him Rover has told me the story and she was going to find out where his mother was and what the real story was , she would ask her mother to talk to the people who were responsible for the animals as they were all animal lovers they would definitely help.

Appu was happy most of the time but in the night he would miss his mother the most as he used to sleep close to her for the warmth , so Bella or Jumbo would make her sleep with them so she was a little comfortable, After a few days Simona came with a few people to the park , after checking the story they had found out because Appu s mother was not well for a long time they had let her go into the forest which was close to the city but you needed a vehicle to go there , the people handling the animals in the zoo had decided to keep Appu but had to let the mother go ,so had separated the mother from the child, now everyone was confused what to do because the mother could be dead.

When Jumbo explained it to Appu , he started crying and said "She told me she will never leave so I am sure she is waiting for me wherever she is ,everyone there who watched Appu cry had tears in their eyes , Bella started explaining to him it would be difficult to find his mother now but he was adamant and said leave me there and I will find her , so the adults explained that they have to get permission to do that but watching his tears they decided to go ahead with the plan of releasing him in the same forest but it would take a few days.

All the animals kept Appu busy with something or the other just to take his mind of his sadness , he would be ok but suddenly he would quietly go to Jumbo and rub him self and stay close to him , all understood his pain ,losing a mother when you are so young could be difficult for anybody .Days passed but he got sadder by the day ,and kept saying his mother would be more sadder as she would be all alone in the forest ,a few more days passed and then one day Simona came in the evening but only spoke to Jumbo after that she said bye to all and went away , all the animals looked at Jumbo waiting for him to say something but he remained quite ,they felt bad for Appu thinking it was bad news .so they quietly took Appu away from there.

The next day it was a beautiful morning as winter was setting in ,it was nice and cool ,the animals were eating their breakfast Appu was eating bananas which he loved the most so he was having a competition with Sonu and Monu as to who could have the most and was winning hands down. ,suddenly Babu came running towards them with a big smile on his face ,he did not say anything just pointed out towards the gate ,all the animals followed him and when they reached the gate they heard a loud trumpet sound and saw a big elephant entering the park they just knew it was Appu's mom and when they turned around to check where he was , they saw him standing still behind staring at her when she sounded the trumpet again he just started running towards her ,It was the most beautiful sight anybody had seen, they kept nuzzling and hugging each other with tears in their eyes. Then he turned around and introduced his mother to all the animals in the park. Everybody was happy for them

They were told it was easy to find her as she was marked by the zoo on her legs and also both the mother and Appu were going to be released to a national park reserve so they could be safe and together there ,

M/S- mothers love is God's blessing on all children, so always love your mother unconditionally

Animal Facts

One day Jumbo, Simba Gaffu and Stripy were sitting together between trees where it was cooler and they were covered by bushes as they were trying to stay away from the sound of fire crackers as it was festival time for the humans, it disturbed them lots specially, Stripy and Gaffu, Simba and Jumbo were in the circus so they had heard these loud crackers, they were discussing the differences among each other but could not understand the reasons but they knew the humans knew the reason because they treated them differently .

Just then Kitty came along looking harassed too but she said Rover is hiding under the bench because it was too loud for him and he can't bear the sound, she sat down and told them that Simona that evening was getting for all of them ear plugs so that it could reduce the sound as this could go on all night. Jumbo asked Kitty if she why knew why they were treated in different ways, she thought for a little while and then said, Jumbo they have seen you before in circuses and Zoos but they are in awe of you, that's why they touch you and want you to tap their head with your trunk I think to get your blessings, they know you are gentle animal, you have a great memory and you always help other animals. Gaffu even you are considered as gentle giant of the jungle you need 10 minutes to two hours of sleep and you can sleep standing up that's why you are awake and taking care of every body who are in trouble in the night , your kindness surprises me a lot. But youll both are the largest animals in the forest but never take advantage of your size.

Simba you are known as the king of the jungles, so they fear you a lot that's why you are always in a cage when you are in a circus or in the Zoo .this is because of what they have heard and seen about you but they don't know you are old now and don't have much teeth, you cant even eat an apple but that we know , not them so let them fear you , all the animals started laughing ,she continued. they don't know you are friendly and so protective of all the animals in the park and your roar can be heard as far as 5 miles away so they don't mess with you.

Kitty lastly looked at the Zebra and said you are from Africa so I have no idea how you got here but everybody knows you here as they make black and white stripes on the roads which is called Zebra crossing for people to cross the roads when there is heavy traffic but you are fast animal I have no idea why but I will check with

Rohan or Simona as they check Google and give me all information but I know no two zebras have the same stripe pattern just like the humans fingerprints so each one of youll are created differently and if one of you'll are in danger all the other zebras come to defend , that's why you are so protective of all of us in the park , every body was so engrossed in all this information when they noticed Bella sitting next to the large tree looking angrily at Kitty she loudly said ' what about me ,do you know any thing about me ,Kitty smiled and said 'you are my friend ,I found out about you first youll love water and are in it for 16 hours a day to cool down but you only get water here when the gardeners are watering the plants but you never complain ,I love you for that but the funny fact about hippos are they don't know to swim .everybody had a smile on their faces but nobody dared to laugh knowing Bella would be upset, so Kitty continued Mother hippos are the most protective and nurturing of their children that's why you look after all the animals in the park ,.,Then Kitty said now I am really tired so enough of information for today ,all stood up and started clapping for Kitty and hugged her and thanked her a lot.

M/S Stop complaining about they way you look and they way you are cause you cant change it ,so just change the way you think because somebody will always love you just the way you are .

www.ingramcontent.com/pod-product-compliance
Lightning Source LLC
LaVergne TN
LVHW061622070526
838199LV00078B/7391